COLLECTION « THÉÂTRE »

The Dragonfly of Chicoutimi
de Larry Tremblay
est le dix-neuvième titre de cette collection.

LARRY TREMBLAY

The Dragonfly of Chicoutimi

théâtre

LES HERBES ROUGES

Éditions Les Herbes rouges
3575, boulevard Saint-Laurent, bureau 304
Montréal (Québec) H2X 2T7
Téléphone : (514) 845-4039
Télécopieur : (514) 845-3629

En première de couverture :
Jean-Louis Millette dans *The Dragonfly of Chicoutimi,*
photo d'Yves Dubé
Photo de l'auteur : Rolf Puls

Distribution : Diffusion Dimedia inc.
539, boulevard Lebeau
Saint-Laurent (Québec) H4N 1S2
Téléphone : (514) 336-3941

Dépôt légal : quatrième trimestre 1995
Bibliothèque nationale du Québec
Bibliothèque nationale du Canada

The Dragonfly of Chicoutimi a été créé en mai 1995, à Montréal, au Théâtre d'Aujourd'hui, dans le cadre du Festival de Théâtre des Amériques. Jean-Louis Millette interprétait le rôle de Gaston Talbot.

Mise en scène : Larry Tremblay
Assistance et régie : Josée Kleinbaum
Scénographie : Mario Bouchard
Éclairage : Michel Beaulieu
Musique originale : Philippe Ménard
Costume : Amaya Clunès
Maquillage : Jacques Lee Pelletier
Direction de production : Harold Bergeron

Une production du Théâtre d'Aujourd'hui
et du Festival de Théâtre des Amériques.

L'auteur remercie Lorraine Hébert, Maureen LaBonté
et David Homel pour leurs précieux commentaires.

The Dragonfly of Chicoutimi was first performed in May of 1995 at the Théâtre d'Aujourd'hui as part of the Festival de Théâtre des Amériques, in Montreal. Jean-Louis Millette played Gaston Talbot.

Director: Larry Tremblay
Assistant to the Director and Stage Manager: Josée Kleinbaum
Set Design: Mario Bouchard
Lighting: Michel Beaulieu
Original Music: Philippe Ménard
Costume Design: Amaya Clunès
Make-up: Jacques Lee Pelletier
Production Manager: Harold Bergeron

Produced by the Théâtre d'Aujourd'hui
and the Festival de Théâtre des Amériques.

The author is grateful to Lorraine Hébert, Maureen LaBonté
and David Homel for their invaluable observations.

Pour David Ley

GASTON TALBOT

I travel a lot
I see a lot of things
very different from what we are used to see here
of course
when we travel we see different things
that's quite sure
but I have the feeling to tell it to repeat it
why
I don't really know
maybe saying it I just want to make a contact
to keep in touch as we say

What a nice expression
TO KEEP IN TOUCH
I like it I love it
I appreciate it so much
really what I'm looking for in life
is to keep in touch

that's the most important thing
and I seriously think that our duty
is to keep in touch
so much people and things are left out
so tonight my motto is
TO KEEP IN TOUCH

Actually
I try my best to keep in touch
with my very close environment
with everything and every person around me
I want to be in not to be out
I want to feel the right thing at the right moment
for the right reason

It's a question of fitting
I just want to fit with the scenery
the world is a bunch of problems
everyone knows that
if we share the same vision
we can handle the world
if we feel the same thing all together
we create a magic moment
and we deserve it after all
we are human beings
we are on earth to improve ourselves
all together we can do something great
and not only great
we can do MAGIC
I love so much that word
it's really a powerful one
I mean love and sharing
are the roots of MAGIC on earth

we don't need anything else

My name is Gaston Talbot
I was born in Chicoutimi
Chicoutimi is an amerindian word
it means up to where the water is deep
this word refers to the Saguenay
a big a beautiful a splendid river
but Chicoutimi as a town is ugly
as every American town
and this ugliness is very interesting
but fortunately nature surrounds every town
in this country
and nature cannot be ugly
right
when I was young
I used to play in the forest near my home
a little forest with a river called rivière aux Roches
this river was full of stones
as if a huge volcano had spit them
my friends and I
went down to the river on those stones
we were not afraid to lose ourselves in the forest
on the contrary we wanted adventures
we considered this charming area of woods
as an Amazonia where wild animals lived
where enormous flowers secreted poisons
where dangerous people watched us
with in their hands deadly weapons
we were frightened
thousands of enemies around us
watching the right moment to catch us
but finally we were always enough strong

to win the battle to kill the bad people
to clean the forest of the evil
o boy o boy o boy
what good memories

My childhood was surely a big success
because of that small piece of forest
near my family house
the freedom I felt down there
was the real root of my strength and my perspicacity
a child came into the forest
walked under the branches of the trees
but a man came out
with in his brain a vision a clear idea of his future
of what he had to do for the sake of his destiny

ONCE UPON A TIME
all my life I always got the dream
to start the story of my life
by saying ONCE UPON A TIME
and now I am ready fully ready to say
without any fear
once upon a time a boy named Gaston Talbot
born in Chicoutimi
in the beautiful province of Quebec
in the great country of Canada
had a dream and that dream came true
does it not sound *bien chic and swell*
that's common sense to answer yeah

Let's start again
once upon a time a boy named Gaston Talbot
played in the little forest

just behind his family house
beside him stood a young boy named Pierre Gagnon

I close my eyes and Pierre appears
he was a bit older than me
how old was I during this period of my life
ten years eleven not very important
let me say that both of us were enough old
to understand all what happened on that specific day
which day
a hot summer day of July
I'm still able to hear the bees around our heads
the sound of the river the songs of the sparrows
the sky was pure blue
naked blue without a single spot of cloud
I'm still able to smell the grass and the wild flowers
burn by the sun
everything was dry except our skin full of sweat
Pierre Gagnon was a beautiful child
blond hair blue eyes round and puffy cheeks
but a bit dumb
his father was not so bright either
he drank and was always on welfare
anyway let's go back to that sunny hot day of July
Pierre and I as all children in the world I presume
loved to play cowboys and Indians
pow pow you're dead that kind of stuff
that day I was the cowboy and Pierre the Indian
I definitely preferred to be the cowboy
and Pierre Gagnon never asked to be that
sometimes with other friends
I was obliged to play the Indian
but with Pierre I was always the cowboy

I presume that he got his fun
dying from the bullet of the cowboy who I was
that sunny day of July
I killed for more than an hour Pierre Gagnon
both of us were exhausted
the sun was incredibly hot
and transformed the forest into a desolated area
a kind of Sahara with carbonized trees
so it was just normal that Pierre and I
went down to the river rivière aux Roches
in search of freshness
Pierre without saying a word
took off all his clothes
got into the river and started to laugh
he looked like a little devil
a cute and joyful devil laughing for nothing
I think he was swallowed
by a strange state of empty happiness
just because he was as I said
a little bit dumb
even if I was very young
my sharp sense of things
my capacity to catch exactly what is going on
under the false appearance of events
put me straight in front of the truth
there was something totally wrong
on that hot sunny day of July
what exactly was it
no doubt that it concerned first
the naked body of Pierre Gagnon
laughing like a fool
in the water of the river rivière aux Roches
in the little forest

just behind my family house

THE NAKED BODY OF PIERRE GAGNON
that sounds very strange for my ears
even now after so many years
look at me
I have white hair
all those wrinkles around my eyes my lips my neck
my skin is yellow
my hands shake my legs hurt me
I have a bad breath
which indicates stomach troubles
I can't eat what I want and so on and so on
my body is a total ruin
but the river rivière aux Roches still flows in my veins
look
I put my hand near my ear
and hear the clear sound of the river
rolling on the rocks
very special this glouglou of the water
you know what I mean
don't you
sometimes
usually when I have to cross the streets
trying to save my life
in that dangerous city where the green light
never lasts enough time for people like me
I hear inside my body
not the water
but the rocks of the river rivière aux Roches
falling down without ever reaching the bottom
the bottom of what
guess

as you can observe
my body is full of surprises full full full

I told you that I travel a lot
that's not true
I told you that just to make me more interesting
it's common sense that people who travel
are more interesting than people
who stay all their life in the same little spot
so I introduced myself as a person who travels a lot
but really it's not true
I spent all my life in Chicoutimi
Chicoutimi which means
up to where the water is shallow
I believe in the power of destiny
to be born in Chicoutimi is very meaningful
up to where it's not profound
think about it
that's something you know

My childhood was a big success
I told you that too
it's not true
well the truth is not easy to catch
for a long time
when I woke up in the morning
I felt so depressed
that all I wanted was to go back to sleep
and sink into the depths of the nothingness
I used then to dream a lot
and one night on two
I was scared to death by nightmares
I was in an awful shape

but one night
I had a dream in English
let's say that it was
if I was blind and suddenly I recovered the sight
or if I was a horse and suddenly I turned into a dog
I know comparison is not reason
however what I want to express
is that the mere fact to dream in English
which after all is something more or less ordinary
even if as for me at that moment of my life
I was a French speaking person
was felt as a dramatic change
or even more
as a signal
something like an angel
coming down to the earth of my consciousness
to show me the way
for all those reasons
I remember precisely
all the details of that dream

Let me describe this dream

In the dream
I was a child
I mean I felt like a child
with an adult body
the body of my forties
the dream began
on Sainte-Anne Street in Chicoutimi
which is divided in two parts
Chicoutimi and Chicoutimi-Nord
the Saguenay separates them

the Sainte-Anne bridge makes the link between them
fifteen years ago they built a second bridge
ugly it goes without saying
beside the old one
the Sainte-Anne bridge nowadays is only for pedestrians
and for people who want to suicide
anyway
the Sainte-Anne Street starts at this bridge
and goes north to south
dividing the town in east and west
my parents rented a house on Sainte-Anne Street
between Saint-Joseph Street and Saint-Dominique Street
there is nothing interesting to say about this area
we are not responsible of the place where we are born
just remember however
that nearby
was the forest of the river rivière aux Roches
where I spent my essential childhood

Back to the dream
I was a child
with an adult body
I was on Sainte-Anne Street
sucking a popsicle
a white popsicle
everyone knows I suppose
the flavor of a white popsicle
I hope so
because it would be very difficult
to find the words to describe this flavor
a kind of coconut taste
but so artificial that it was impossible
to find out the stuff they use

to make my favorite popsicle
so I was sucking on Sainte-Anne Street
this white popsicle
when suddenly I had nothing more to suck
the popsicle simply disappeared
I had in my mouth only the wooden stick
the popsicle didn't fall down on the sidewalk
as it happened so often when I was a child
it just disappeared
like a bird or a flower is made disappeared
by the quick hands of a magician
I wasn't impressed at all by this disparition
I said
my popsicle disappeared so what
I said that in English
and I wasn't at all impressed
by the fact I said that in English
I was a child
with an adult body
speaking in English
so what

Back again to the dream
so I had in my hand
only the wooden stick of the popsicle
but after a short while
I had two sticks in my hand
and after another short while
three sticks and pow pow pow
I had ten or more sticks
I said
what a lucky boy I am
all these popsicle wooden sticks just for me

I have here to explain something
I'm an artist
in a way
I made an Eiffel tower
I made an Olympic stadium
I made big plates for fruits
I made a ship Japanese style
I made a Star Trek vessel
I even tried to make a human face
but I failed
anyway I got so much success
with my houses and their stairways
maybe a total of two hundred pieces
the biggest one has six feet high
that's something you know
and all that with simple wooden popsicle sticks
plus a bit of white glue
I was about twelve or thirteen
when I began to pick up on the sidewalks
and in the schoolyards
the popsicle sticks
to make my masterpieces
I stopped to do so in my thirties
two years ago I started again
for me now it's crucial to make things
with popsicle sticks
it makes me feel good
it makes me feel right
I mean I feel connected with the world
when I get up at five in the morning
wash myself eat an apple or corn flakes
dress myself go out in the streets still deserted
in search of popsicle sticks

I feel great

Sometimes strange thoughts crossed my mind
example
if I had seen during the day
a pregnant woman on the street
at night lying down in my bed
I spoke to myself in the following manner
this woman has a baby in her belly
nobody can see the baby
it's a hidden body
but me
in my bed
I could imagine the moment when the baby
seven or eight years later
would be a child playing with his friends
asking money to his mother to buy candy
and surely POPSICLES
and me I would be there
ready to pick up the stick
that he would surely throw away
never children throw their popsicle sticks in the garbage
never
and it's okay for me

Let's go back to the dream
I was on Sainte-Anne Street
in Chicoutimi
which means up to where the ships can go
and for the very first time in my life
I said something in a pure and understandable English
I said
my popsicle disappeared so what

and indeed so what
but I have to put it clear
the boy I was in my dream was not me
I mean he looked like me
if we consider that it was me
as a child with an adult body
but
and there is always a but
his face oh his face
this face was not mine
a strange mix in fact
it's a question of look anyway
everything in that superficial world
is a bloody question of look
am I right
oh yeah I am
I don't want to give the idea
that I'm a real connoisseur in the field of arts
but I have got some knowledge about painting
I know by heart some big names
Van Gogh Chagall Gauguin and Picasso
let me tell you
the face of the boy in my dream
which is supposed to be mine
looked exactly like a face of a Picasso
you get the picture
the nostrils are on the top of the nose
the mouth touches the forehead
and you can see simultaneously the face and the profile
all you can say is that something is wrong
so when I said in the dream
my popsicle disappeared so what
I got a look at my own face

and that face was a real Picasso
and when all these popsicle sticks
appeared from my shaking hands
this Picasso face looked at me with a strange smile
and something cruel in the eyes
for the sake of God
who is he
who is looking at me
with my own face
who is smiling at me
with my own smile
I started to run on Sainte-Anne Street
but I ran with that funny face on my shoulders
I understood that to run away was not a solution
how could I get rid of it
after a short while
I stood before the front door of my family home
at the 640 Sainte-Anne Street
I knocked the door
that's stupid I know
we have not to knock the door
where we live
but I'm just trying to describe my dream
as it came to me
I knocked
toc toc toc
no answer
I knocked again
it's me mum
your beloved son
I need your help
it's time for you
to show me your love

I'm in trouble
guess what happened to me
mum mum
open your heart
let me get in
give me your arms
protect me against the evil
look at the flesh of your own flesh

I need a break

I failed

It's not good
it's not at all good

What a pity
I'm not able to tell the truth
the naked truth
the simple and undressed truth
mother of all possibilities

Picasso
that's not true
I didn't get a Picasso face
not for a second

I was on Sainte-Anne Street in Chicoutimi
which means where the city stops or starts
with an adult body and an heart of a child
and the face of Pierre Gagnon on my shoulders
the popsicle sticks in my hands
transformed themselves into stones

each time I threw one on the ground
one more immediately appeared to replace it
I panicked
I ran as quick as possible
at 640 Sainte-Anne Street
knocked the door
mum mum
it's me
your terrible son
I hate geniuses
I hate people who think
we are dummies
who think that we will admire
a piece of shit
on a white sheet
because they put their name on it
I'm an artist
not a Picasso
I'm not creating monsters
I'm not selling my shit
nobody loves me
nobody touches me
I'm alone
I'm a terrible man
when I get up in the morning
I go outside
looking for popsicle sticks
this is a life
a real and tough life
mum mum
open the fucking door
I'll kill you
you understand me

open the fucking door
look at your son of a bitch
don't let him shout in the streets
look mum
look at the blood
look at the hands
look at the stones
it's magic
pure magic
I throw a stone
another one appears right after
my hands are full of stones from rivière aux Roches

Now I will play the part of mum

I have a cotton dress
an awful but so secure polka dot dress
I have my hair tied in a horse tail
I wear no make-up
my skin is white
like a pint of milk
I'm big I'm fat
but I have beautiful brown eyes
I don't hear my son
calling for me outside the door
I hear nothing
it's not my dream after all
and I'm not supposed to be there
so my son knocks and knocks
on that fucking door
and I don't give a damn
I'm going now to make a chocolate cake

No mum
don't let me down
don't make a chocolate cake
open your arms
for the cute baby I am
make a window in the door
and have a look
I'm naked
I mean
I have no more stones

Go away son of a bitch

You are not supposed
to speak like this
you are an official mum

Let's make a deal
come back
when I'll finish my chocolate cake

No mum
I want you now

I woke up went to pee
looked at my face in the mirror
Pierre Gagnon
why are you doing that to me
please stay quiet
stay in your place
in the gentle waves of the river rivière aux Roches
don't take my face
it belongs to my mother

I went back to my bed
slept and dreamed again

Now the door is open
how
I don't know

I smell something
chocolate cake
my heartbeats increase
make noise in my mouth
I hear the radio coming from the kitchen
a song
I know that song
tout va très bien Madame la marquise
tout va très bien tout va très bien
I walk a few steps
the floor is wet
I say to myself
it's Friday
mum always washes the floor on Friday
I'm happy and sad
I love Friday
but I hate fish
I look my hands
the stones are gone
no more magic
I feel released
for now I just want to go
straight in the kitchen
open the freezer
and take a popsicle
a white one

mum always makes grocery on Friday
I'm sure
there is some popsicles in the freezer
my heartbeats still increase
boum boum
mum buys popsicles on Friday
but I have to wait Saturday to have them

Time
it's a question of time
I hate time
my dream won't last forever

Why mum is doing a cake

Why mum closed the door

Those questions strangle me

Back to mum

I wear an apron
over my cotton dress
I have still my hair
tied in a horse tail
I'm big fat and beautiful
I put on lipstick
a crude violent red
I say to myself
my lips are cherries
my white skin is bread
my heart is a chocolate cake
for the birthday of my beloved son

I have nine children
five boys four girls
I give them all my love
and this love
is separated in nine equal parts
by the knife of motherhood
but Gaston is different
he's so fragile so naive
he needs more than his part
oh Gaston please
take all the cake
I'm preparing
for the birthday of your seven years
but don't come now
stay behind the door
it's not ready yet
you understand
you son of a bitch
it's a surprise
Tout va très bien Madame la marquise
tout va très bien tout va très bien

This dream will kill me again
shall I go through with it
I shall
why

Back to mum
oh I'm so delighted
to have given birth
to such an adorable son
let me show you
his photo taken at his first birthday

cute isn't he
look at these brown eyes
my eyes
look at this nose
my nose
look at this mouth
my mouth
that's why I put so much love
in the chocolate cake
son of a bitch
are you there
don't come
it's almost ready
I have still to put
on the cake your seven candles
it's a surprise
don't forget

Now I know
what is going on here
it's my birthday
my heartbeats increase more
in a few seconds
I will have to blow my candles
will I be able to
and what will be my wish
those questions strangle me

What a nightmare
I suddenly discover
that I have no wish

Back to mum

I'm not a real mum
with heart and bosom
apron and lipstick
but for Gaston
on that very special day
at the question
will you be the loving mother of that boy
I will answer yes
let's prepare our mouth
for singing
happy birthday Gaston
let's prepare our smile
to put a real sense of music
in that stupid song
beloved son
come
the surprise is ready
candles don't last forever

Back to me

As I said
I'm a child
with an adult body
the floor is wet
my heart is on the edge of exploding
I don't think anymore
about white popsicles
I fix my mind
on that terrible thought
in a few seconds
I will blow my candles
without a wish

I make a step forward
come into the kitchen
it's dark
the light is off

Hi mum
let's kiss each other

You're right son
let's kiss

Your lips taste wild cherries

Please don't mention it

Oh mum
this chocolate cake is just for me

You're right son
look
you will see my heart
burning in the middle of the candles

Great

Happy birthday Gaston
now blow

I sweat as a pig
how can I blow without a wish
my life is definitely in ruins

Blow

The arms of mum
are big fat and beautiful
but also very strong
they grasp my head
push it over the flames of the seven candles
I feel the heat burning the hairs of my nostrils
the saliva drying at the corner of my lips
in a second
my heart will explode
my face will be in fire
if I don't blow
these fucking candles
so I blow them
wishing not to die

Mum hugs me
the radio still sings
tout va très bien Madame la marquise
tout va très bien tout va très bien
mum turns on the light
turns herself toward me
to present me the knife
to cut the astonishing chocolate cake
where her heart beats
surrounded by hot wax drops
but when she looks at my face
in the yellow light of the 100 watt bulb
of the kitchen
all her hair including the horse tail
rises into the air as if her body is crossed
by a tremendous electrical shock

I say to myself

what's the matter
the ceiling is sucking mum up
her lip is rolled up
showing teeth like a mad dog

Who are you
you're not my beloved son
that nose is not mine
those blue eyes
are not my brown eyes
and what this fucking blond hair
is doing in my kitchen
don't touch the cake

For my own unhappiness
here I don't get the reflex to wake up
my dream goes on
without my agreement
and it gives mum
all the time she wants
to run after me
a knife in her right hand

Are you nuts
cut the cake
don't cut me

I repeat

Are you nuts
cut the cake
don't cut me

But mum is on her way
nothing can stop her
you know the strength
and the inflexibility of a mother
therefore this dream transforms itself
undoubtedly into a nightmare
at the precise instant
when mum throws the knife
and successfully reaches her target
tout va très bien Madame la marquise
tout va très bien tout va très bien

A dragonfly fixed on a wall by a pin
I saw one once
I had an uncle who got crazy for insects
he showed me his collection
I was very young
maybe three or four years
I thought that the insects were all alive
fixed in a posture
on the starting line
waiting for the signal
which will allow them to fly away in all directions
when my uncle showed me
his enormous dragonfly
I was so attracted by it
that I touched it
but my move was too quick
the pin where the insect was fixed pricked me
blood came out at the tip of my finger
my uncle ran to it and sucked the blood
for many years
I thought that the dragonfly bit me

with his mouth or with his jaw or whatever

When the knife thrown by mum
transpierced my chest
fixing my body on the yellow wall of the kitchen
it was impossible for me to escape
the sensation and the idea
I was nothing but
a dragonfly fixed on a wall by a pin

Who are you

I'm the flesh of your flesh
look at me
touch me
please give me your help
I don't want to be an insect
I want to go to school
to learn French math
geography history of Canada
I want to eat mashed potatoes
steak and suck white popsicles

Nonsense
I recognize you now
you are Pierre Gagnon
the dumb child

Don't believe that
you are under the influence of my dream
don't buy anything here
remember the story of the prince and the frog

Don't try to catch me
with child's stories

Please kiss me
you will see
the prince your son
behind this awful mask

I don't kiss shit
I'm a true mother
one hundred per cent
made with love perfume
apron rings lipstick
chocolate cake and candles
my heart is tender
as a field of new grass
I gave birth
to nine sumptuous children
and Gaston is the jewel of that crown
which squeezes my head to death

A kiss
just a little one

Never
and now die
since your blood
is almost covering my floor

How can I die
my dream
even if it's a nightmare
will never allow my own death

Prove it

What

Prove that is your dream

Mum
it's obvious

Bullshit

Okay I will prove it to you
choose a number
I will guess it
since it's my dream
whatever you get inside your brain
it's already in mine
after all
your brain is nothing but
a tiny ball lost in my brain
you get your number

Sure

Okay
now I need a bit of silence
will you be kind enough
to turn off the radio
I cannot concentrate myself
with that « *tout va très bien Madame la marquise* »
in background
thank you mum

Don't call me so

Please stay in front of me
don't move
I need to look in your eyes

Shit and bullshit

Please be kind

Guess the number
I'm in a hurry
do you think
I will let you transform my kitchen floor
into a vulgar red sea

It's your fault
you gave me life
with your blood
don't you smell it

Guess the number

It's coming oh it's coming
now I see the number
indeed I see two numbers
one in each eye
will you be kind enough mum
to concentrate yourself
on one number only

That's what I'm doing from the beginning

False
and now you are changing everything
how could I catch the number
if you change your mind every second

You are silly Pierre Gagnon

I'm not Pierre Gagnon
and stop to make me confused
now you are counting
6 7 8 9 10 11
that's not fair

Nonsense and pure bullshit
from the beginning
I have my mind fixed
on one and only one number

Impossible
and please be kind with your beloved son
after all I'm dying
don't you feel sorry
a bit of compassion
would be appreciated here
and let's put an end to all this shit
I'm fed up of that dirty kitchen
I'm fed up of loosing my blood on the floor
I'm fed up of you mum
looking at me as a stranger
KISS ME

She did

A quick kiss
on my left cheek

Suddenly
the Picasso's mask or whatever
fell down from my face
showing a dragonfly's head
mum cried like death
I opened up my big jaws
and I ate ate ate
the body of mum
from head to toes
hair and shoes included
excited by this incestuous meal
I swallowed the chocolate cake
with its seven candles
making the wish to fly

My wish was instantly fulfilled
the roof of my family house
exploded like a Coke cap
under the press of its shaked bottle
and I was pushed by an inner geyser
out of the kitchen
for the very first time of my life
I knew what was the meaning of happiness

I need a break

Happiness
that's not the point
I'm definitely not happy
look at my face

look
do you feel
the horrible tempo of my heart
it could be worse I know
everything could be worse
without any help
but I have a bad smell
do you smell it
do you identify it
a bad look a bad smell
and a hundred per cent bad luck
I Gaston Talbot
spent almost all my time
picking up on streets
popsicle sticks
to make not art as I said
but ready-made shit
garbage of a poor soul

Oh Pierre Gagnon
I never said
never never said
that your body
was the only one I ever touched

Happiness
bullshit for birds
for people with cars and houses
not for Gaston
not for that dumb Chicoutimi boy

Once upon a time
Gaston Talbot

a dragonfly who ate his mother
the day of his seven years
flew into the sky of Chicoutimi
for the first time of his life
the sight of his native place
made him happy
indeed he was euphoric
he saw with his eyes washed by the wind
the joyful pattern of the roofs
strange cattle scattered
in the crude green of the pines
in the yellow of the fields
he saw the quivering waves of the Saguenay
making their way through the rock of the fjord
like a liquid knife sculpting the landscape
he made a dive over Racine Street
increased his speed and in an acrobatic loop
returned to the infinite freedom of the sky
he felt amazingly beautiful powerful
faster than the speed of wind
unreachable and untouchable
with his lungs filled forever
with a courage of steel
when he threw a quick eye
on the little stream of the river rivière aux Roches
a strange attraction
obliged him to go down more and more
toward the tiny bright vein of the river
he could do nothing against this attraction
in a few seconds
he will crash
he tried desperately
to move his four dragonfly's wings

but he suddenly was aware
that he was simply shaking in the air
two stupid arms
he clearly understood
that it was the end
in a moment
he would be dead
crushed on the rocks of the river rivière aux Roches

BOUM

Dream is over

I wake up
totally wet
I open my eyes
I'm not in my bed
I'm lying on a body
a cold and wet body
the dead body of Pierre Gagnon
my lips are on his lips
I'm doing a mouth-to-mouth
I'm touching his blond hair
I'm looking his blue and fixed eyes
I'm taking his head with my two hands
and crushing it on the rocks
the blood of Pierre Gagnon
reddens the water of the river rivière aux Roches

What I told you
about those days spent to play with Pierre Gagnon
cowboys and Indians
in the little forest near my home

is not totally true
in fact I was the Indian
and Pierre the cowboy
he was about twelve years old
I was four years more than him
but I was so dumb
and he was so bright
he was the one
who knew what to do
at the right moment
for the right reason
he was the one
who deserved to be the glorious cowboy

Pierre's real name
was Pierre Gagnon-Connally
his mother Huguette Gagnon
married Major Tom Connally
he was from Windsor
he came to Saguenay
to work on the military base of Bagotville
Pierre always said to me
that his father was a pilot
he was so proud of him
but I never believed that
he was probably mechanic or operator
when Pierre was about ten
his parents divorced
his father left Bagotville

On that hot sunny day of July
Pierre Gagnon-Connally asks me to be his horse
I say yes

I stop being the Indian
I start to behave like a horse
I make noise with my lips
I jump I run everywhere
Pierre Gagnon-Connally catches me
with an invisible lasso
inserts in my mouth an invisible bit
and jumps on my back
he rides me guiding me with his hands on my hair
after a while he gets down from my back
looks at me as he never did before
then he starts to give me orders in English

I don't know English
but on that hot sunny day of July
every word which comes
from the mouth of Pierre Gagnon-Connally
is clearly understandable

Get rid of your clothes

Yes sir

Faster faster

Pierre Gagnon-Connally
removes from his pocket a cigarette
he lights it smokes it

Get down on your knees
you're a horse
not a man

Yes sir

He approaches me
puts out his cigarette on my thigh

Now you belong to me
you got my mark

Yes sir

Don't talk
a horse doesn't talk

I neigh

Eat now

I eat the grass

Good horse
come here now

He climbs on my back

Go to the river

I know where is the river
but Pierre never stops giving me orders

Go straight
turn left
left again
turn right

go straight
faster faster
son of a bitch
here we are
drink now

I drink
Pierre Gagnon-Connally on my back

Good horse
drink again
we have still a long ride to go

I drink again
looking my broken face
reflected in the water
of the river rivière aux Roches
but suddenly
I stand up
with the strength and the surprise of a spring
projecting Pierre in the river
I turn back
I see his broken body on the rocks

Silence appears
it's the air itself

I touch his body
I feel his life
I do a mouth-to-mouth
I see so close his face
I can't handle it
I take his head with my hands

and crush it on the rocks

It was not Pierre who laughed
in the water of the river rivière aux Roches

Nobody never learned
what really happened
on that hot sunny day of July
it was so easy
to think that Pierre slipped on the wet rocks
but if a boy
dumb but a boy
came in the forest on that day
I don't know who came out
specialists who examined me after the accident
declared me aphasic
for years and years
no words came from my mouth
I think I was not
as they said
aphasic
I was simply silent

And years and years later
the dream came
that funny dream I described to you
I told you
that I had this dream in English
and to quote myself
I felt that as a dramatic change
as an alert signal
something like an angel
coming down to the earth of my consciousness

to show me the way
bullshit
total and pure bullshit
why am I a liar like this
why am I so ridiculous
so pitiful
do I deserve
this ugly face you see
this awful voice you hear
do I

The night I had
that dream in English
my mouth was a hole of shit
I mean
full of words like
chocolate cake beloved son
son of a bitch popsicle sticks
your lips taste wild cherries
a dragonfly fixed on a wall by a pin
when the sunlight reached
my dirty sheets my eyes filled with sweat
my mouth was still spitting
all those fucking words
like rotten seeds
everywhere in the room
I was not
as they said
aphasic
anymore
I was speaking in English.

> *Gaston Talbot chante, après en avoir cherché*
> *les mots dans sa mémoire, la chanson «J'at-*

tendrai», popularisée par Tino Rossi.

Gaston Talbot sings, after searching in his memory for the words, "J'attendrai", a song made popular by Tino Rossi.

Postface

Afterword

To Keep in Touch
par Paul Lefebvre

Cette pièce est écrite en anglais. En fait, elle est écrite en français, mais avec des mots anglais. Et dans *The Dragonfly of Chicoutimi,* ce passage linguistique est à la fois sujet et métaphore.

We are not responsible of the place where we are born

Il y a des périodes de l'histoire où une langue domine les autres, devient la *lingua franca* qui permet aux peuples *barbares* de communiquer entre eux et de communiquer avec le peuple qui les assujettit. Le latin, sous la *pax romana,* était une telle langue.

Aujourd'hui, en cette fin du vingtième siècle, l'anglais domine la planète comme aucune langue ne l'a jamais dominée. L'Angleterre, au siècle dernier, a imposé sa langue à tout son empire colonial. Depuis la Seconde Guerre mondiale, les États-Unis ont imposé l'anglais grâce à leur puissance économique et à leur envahissante industrie du divertissement. L'anglais constitue un immense territoire en expansion.

To Keep in Touch
by Paul Lefebvre

This play was written in English. Actually, it was written in French, but using English words. And for *The Dragonfly of Chicoutimi*, this linguistic transfer constitutes both subject and metaphor.

We are not responsible of the place where we are born

There are periods in history when one language dominates other languages, becoming the *lingua franca* which enables the *barbaric* nations to communicate with one another and with their rulers. Under the *pax romana*, Latin was such a language.

Today, at the end of the twentieth century, the English language governs the planet as has no other language before it. A century ago, England imposed its language on all its colonies. Since the end of World War II, the United States has maintained the dominance of English thanks to that country's economic power and to the expansive nature of its entertainment industry. The already huge territory of the English language is still expanding.

Le Québec, îlot francophone encerclé par trois cent millions d'anglophones, a appris que le mot *autre* ne peut s'écrire qu'au singulier, et avec un grand A. Or, en ce moment, cette croyance est en train de se répandre chez tous les peuples, dans toutes les langues. Le grand Autre anglo-saxon est en train d'avaler tous les autres.

> *if we share the same vision*
> *we can handle the world*
> *if we feel the same thing all together*
> *we create a magic moment*

Il est épuisant de résister. Il est épuisant de vouloir être soi face au grand Autre dont la force séduit, attire, même si cet Autre nous nie par indifférence. Même si cet Autre nous opprime, confondant en toute innocence ses intérêts et les nôtres. L'Autre n'a que faire des différences.

À l'intérieur de chaque résistant, il y a une petite voix qui le supplie de se fondre enfin à cette puissance qui l'écrase. Quel Québécois n'a pas songé un jour à cesser de parler français pour renaître dans les eaux de la grande mer anglophone? Obéir au mépris de soi que nous a communiqué l'Autre pour enfin se fusionner à lui? Faire partie de l'Autre pour qu'il n'y ait plus jamais d'autres? Haïr la différence? Comme Gaston Talbot, rêver d'un monde sans clivage aucun, débarrassé de toute expérience d'altérité, d'un monde où toute différence est abolie au profit d'un éternel *magic moment*?

> *I want to be in not to be out*

Gaston Talbot, né à Chicoutimi, est né *out*. Et cet incident de sexe et de domination et de langue anglaise et de mort avec THE NAKED BODY OF PIERRE

Quebec, an enclave of six million Francophones surrounded by a mass of three hundred million Anglophones,
has learned that the word *other* can only be written in the
singular, and with a capital O. This belief is spreading to
most other nations, to all other languages. The great Anglo-
Saxon Other is swallowing up all the others.

if we share the same vision
we can handle the world
if we feel the same thing all together
we create a magic moment

It's exhausting to resist all the time. It's exhausting to
want to remain oneself despite the great Other, whose
strength is seductive, enticing; even though the Other in-
validates us through indifference; even though the Other
oppresses us, by inadvertently mistaking its interest for our
own. The Other has no use for differences.

Inside every resistance fighter is a small voice im-
ploring him at least to join forces with the power that's
destroying him. What Québécois has not dreamed of one
day ceasing to speak French, of being re-born into the
great family of the English-speaking majority? Dreamed
one day that he could submit to the self-loathing instilled
in him by the great Other, so as at last to be united with
his master? Wished to be one with the Other, wished there
would never again by any others? Wished he could hate
the difference? To dream, like Gaston Talbot, of a world
without distinction, free from all experience of otherness,
a world where all differences would be abolished in the
name of an eternal *magic moment*?

I want to be in not to be out

Gaston Talbot, born in Chicoutimi, was born *out*. And
this incident of sex and domination, of the English lan-

GAGNON l'a exilé de sa propre vie. Tout traumatisme sexuel fait éclater pour le sujet l'unité du monde, cesse d'en faire un lieu évident, allant de soi. Le sujet n'a pas grand choix : ou bien il se campe orgueilleusement en marge de la majorité sociale, ou bien il tente de trouver un moyen de recoller le miroir éclaté, de réintégrer le corps social, là où, de nouveau, tout irait de soi : *I want to be in not to be out.* Kafka nous a indiqué comment vivre au vingtième siècle : «Dans le combat entre toi et le monde, seconde le monde.» Juif pragois, parlant yiddish dans une ville tchèque, Kafka a entrepris d'écrire son œuvre en allemand.

> *I had a dream in English*
> *let's say that it was*
> *if I was blind and suddenly I recovered the sight*

C'est le rêve, c'est l'inconscient qui dicte à Gaston Talbot la solution. Beckett l'avait compris : si l'on veut se projeter dans une vie fictive, il vaut mieux changer de langue. Il passa au français parce qu'écrire en anglais à partir de choses vécues en anglais, c'était trop douloureux. De son propre aveu, cela aurait rendu l'écriture trop «sentimentale». Se détacher de sa langue : une façon de KEEP IN TOUCH sans que les mots ne nous entraînent dans une agonie sans fin.

Même dans une autre langue, les mots ne peuvent s'empêcher de traquer les douleurs de la vie. L'anglais de Gaston est fragile. En fait, il parle encore et toujours en français, mais avec des mots anglais. Au mieux, les anglophones trouveront que son expression est poétique. Il ne cesse de créer des remparts de mots pour tenir sa vie à distance. Mais les remparts s'écroulent les

guage and death with THE NAKED BODY OF PIERRE GAGNON has exiled him from his own life. Any sexual trauma shatters one's unity with the world, bringing to an end its unquestioned aspect, its obviousness. The human subject has little choice: either he positions himself proudly on the margin of society, or he tries to find a way to put back together the pieces of the broken mirror, to return to the body of society in a way that will make everything right again: *I want to be in not to be out.* Kafka has already shown us how to live in the twentieth century: "In the combat between yourself and the world, assist the world." A Jew from Prague, speaking Yiddish in a Czech city, Kafka decided to write in German.

> *I had a dream in English*
> *let's say that it was*
> *if I was blind and suddenly I recovered the sight*

It's the dream, it's the subconscious that dictates a solution for Gaston Talbot. It was something Beckett had understood: if one wishes to project oneself into a fictitious life, it's best to change languages. Beckett changed from English to French, because writing in English would have been far too painful. As he himself put it, it would have made the writing too "sentimental". And so, detaching oneself from one's own language is a way TO KEEP IN TOUCH without having the words bring about one's endless agony.

Even in a different language, words can't help but track down the pain of life. Gaston's English is fragile. In fact, he is still speaking French, but using English words. At best, English-speaking spectators or readers will find his expression poetic. He constantly builds walls of words as a way of keeping his life at a distance. But the walls

uns après les autres. Et les mots, malgré la distance de
la langue, cernent impitoyablement sa vie.

Fallait-il s'appeler Larry Tremblay et porter dans son
nom les deux langues pour écrire un tel texte, comme si
Larry donnait des mots au silence de *Tremblay*? Fallait-
il être né au Saguenay? Cela a pu faire naître le texte
plus vite. Mais, tôt ou tard, on l'aurait écrit ailleurs, à
Athènes ou à Düsseldorf ou Dieu sait où. D'ailleurs, pour
traduire la pièce en grec ou en allemand, il ne faudrait
pas la mettre en mots grecs ni allemands. Il faudrait
mettre des mots anglais sur une langue grecque ou alle-
mande ; ou lettone, bengali, néerlandaise... Gaston
Talbot, le personnage du *Dragonfly of Chicoutimi,* est
un précurseur.

tumble down, one after another. And the words, despite the distance created by the English language, implacably surround his life.

Must one have the name Larry Tremblay, a name that contains the two languages, in order to create such a text, as if *Larry* has found words for *Tremblay's* silence? Does he have to have been born in the Saguenay region of Quebec? That might have speeded up the birth of such a text. But it seems that sooner or later, an equivalent text would have been written in an equivalent place, Athens maybe, or Düsseldorf, or who knows where else. And of course, to translate the text into Greek or German, one wouldn't have to put it into Greek or German words. One would have to put English words over the Greek or German language; the same would be true for the Lettish, the Bengali, or the Dutch language... Gaston Talbot, the character in *The Dragonfly of Chicoutimi,* is a forerunner.

*Cet ouvrage a été achevé d'imprimer
aux ateliers d'AGMV inc.
à Cap-Saint-Ignace en novembre 1995
pour le compte des
Éditions Les Herbes rouges*

Imprimé au Québec (Canada)

F398